FROM SEA to SHINING SEA

IOWA

DYNISE BALCAVAGE

Consultants

MELISSA N. MATUSEVICH, PH.D.

Curriculum and Instruction Specialist
Blacksburg, Virginia

MARILYN TILLEY

Children's Coordinator
Churdan Public Library
Churdan, Iowa

SUE TEUTSCH

Children's Services
Gibson Memorial Library
Creston, Iowa

CHILDREN'S PRESS®

A DIVISION OF SCHOLASTIC INC.

New York • Toronto • London • Auckland • Sydney • Mexico City
New Delhi • Hong Kong • Danbury, Connecticut

Iowa is in the midwestern part of the United States. It is bordered by Minnesota, Wisconsin, Illinois, Missouri, Nebraska, and South Dakota.

The front cover photograph shows a farm in Iowa's Kossuth County.

Project Editor: Meredith DeSousa
Art Director: Marie O'Neill
Photo Researcher: Marybeth Kavanagh
Design: Robin West, Ox and Company, Inc.
Page 6 map and recipe art: Susan Hunt Yule
All other maps: XNR Productions, Inc.

Library of Congress Cataloging-in-Publication Data

Balcavage, Dynise.
    Iowa / Dynise Balcavage.
      p. cm. – (From sea to shining sea)
    Includes bibliographical references (p.) and index.
    ISBN 0-516-22481-6
    1.Iowa—Juvenile literature. [1. Iowa.] I. Title. II. From sea to shining sea
(Series)

F621.3 .B35 2002
977.7—dc21   2001006981

TABLE of CONTENTS

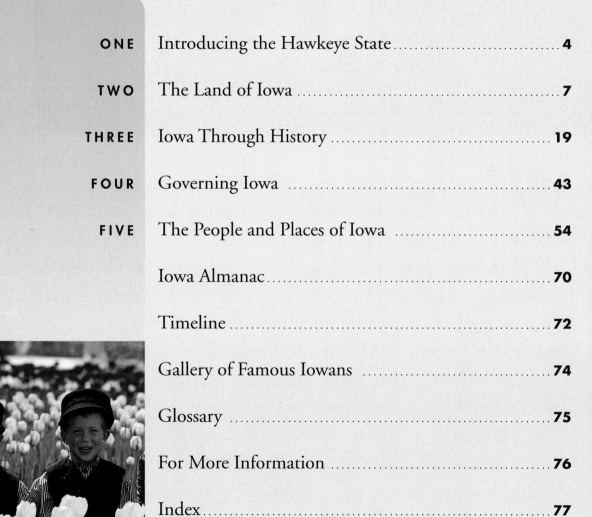

CHAPTER ONE

INTRODUCING THE HAWKEYE STATE

Runners enjoy the scenery along Heritage Trail, a recreational trail that leads to Dubuque.

When you think of Iowa, you probably picture a huge cornfield. This is not surprising. About one in every five pieces of corn that you eat comes from this midwestern state. Iowans also use this tasty grain to make other food products including cereals, breads, and a favorite snack—corn chips. The state's unofficial nicknames, Land Where the Tall Corn Grows, the Corn State, and the Nation's Breadbasket, show how important this crop is to Iowans.

Not all of Iowa is a cornfield. Iowa also has large, bustling cities. Besides employing many workers in industries such as insurance, computers, and technology, cities such as Des Moines and Cedar Rapids also serve as artistic and cultural centers. Iowans often spend weekends watching dance and music performances and visiting museums. People from all over the country visit Des Moines in August to attend its fun-filled state fair.

Native Americans were first to make their home in Iowa. In fact, the name Iowa honors the state's early settlers, the Iowa tribe. The word *Iowa* means "sleepy ones" or "this is the place."

With its rolling hills, rich farmland, and mighty rivers, it's easy to see why the Iowa tribe decided to live in this area. The landscape ranges from the crystal blue Mississippi and Missouri Rivers and lush green hills, to golden fields of grain and chocolate brown earth. Thanks to its beautiful scenery, many movies were filmed in the Hawkeye State, including the popular movie about baseball called *Field of Dreams*.

Iowa is more than just a beautiful landscape. Many well-known writers, including Flannery O'Connor, William Carver, and James Irving, have studied at the Iowa Writers' Workshop. Artist Grant Wood gained fame by painting Iowa farm scenes and landscapes. President Herbert Hoover and author Laura Ingalls Wilder lived in Iowa.

What else comes to mind when you think of Iowa?

❖ The Iowa Hawkeyes football team and the Iowa State Cyclones
❖ Long rows of corn and soybeans
❖ The world's largest tractor factory in Waterloo
❖ Animal-shaped sculptures made long ago by Native Americans
❖ Riverboats paddling down the Mississippi and Missouri Rivers
❖ Des Moines skyscrapers twinkling at dusk
❖ Chief Black Hawk, for whom the state is nicknamed

In this book, you will read about the lives of Iowans and the history of their vibrant state. You will discover the many hidden treasures of the Hawkeye State.

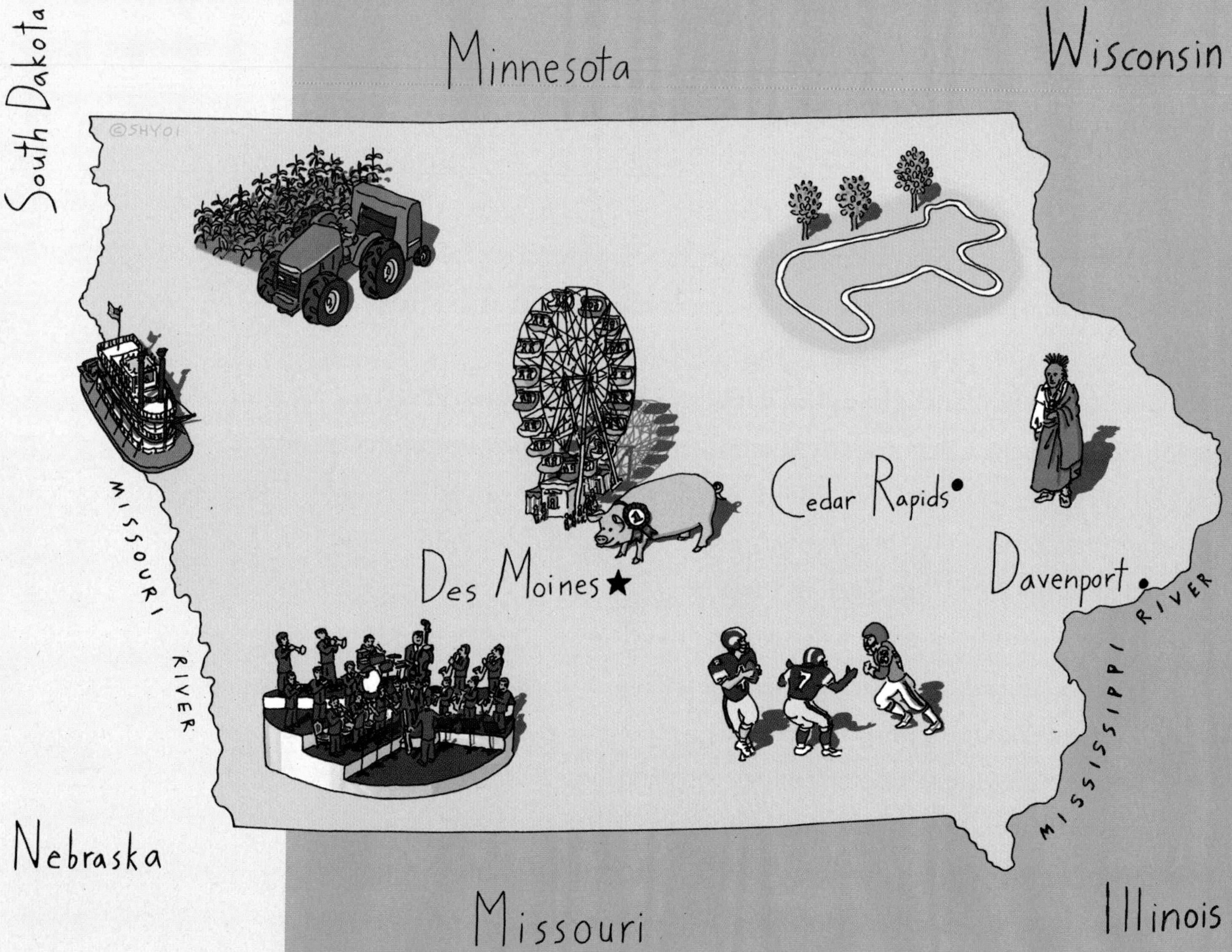

South Dakota

Minnesota

Wisconsin

@SHY01

MISSOURI RIVER

Nebraska

Cedar Rapids●

Des Moines ★

Davenport ●

MISSISSIPPI RIVER

Missouri

Illinois

CHAPTER TWO

THE LAND OF IOWA

Iowa is in the midwestern United States. This area is often called "the heartland," because it is in the center of the country. People in the Midwest also have a reputation for being very friendly and having good hearts.

Iowa is situated between two of the nation's great rivers—the Mississippi River to the east and the Missouri River to the west. Iowa's neighboring states include Illinois and Wisconsin to the east, and South Dakota and Nebraska to the west. Missouri is Iowa's southern neighbor, and Minnesota lies to the north. Some people think Iowa looks like a tiny version of the mainland United States.

Although the greater part of Iowa is level land, Iowa's elevation, or height above sea level, increases as you travel northwest. The state's highest point is on a farm near the Iowa-Minnesota border. This spot rises 1,670 feet (509 meters) above sea level.

The Des Moines River flows south through Iowa before emptying into the Mississippi River.

Two million years ago, four giant sheets of ice, or glaciers, covered present-day Iowa. These ice sheets were about one mile (1.6 kilometers) thick. They "ironed out" most of the land into a flat plain. The last trace of ice in Iowa melted about 11,000 years ago.

From flat to hilly, dotted with lakes and framed by two mighty rivers, Iowa has many different landscapes. It is divided into three geographic regions: the Dissected Till Plains, the Young Drift Plains, and the Driftless Area.

Dissected Till Plains

When Iowa's first glaciers melted, they left beds of rock and soil called till on the plains. Thousands of years after the glaciers melted, many brooks and streams flowed across the flat land. The nonstop force of the moving water caused rolling hills and ridges to dissect, or cut apart, the plains. Strong winds then sprinkled the till across these gentle hills.

Today, southern Iowa and parts of northwestern Iowa near the Missouri and Big Sioux Rivers make up a region called the dissected till plains. The rich soil there is very good for farming. Not surprisingly, this part of Iowa is dotted with farms.

The till also gave Iowa one especially beautiful landmark. The state's Loess (pro-

FIND OUT MORE

The ground in southeast Iowa is scattered with rocks called geodes. These rocks have a dull, gray shell, but if you crack them open, you will find colorful crystals inside. How did geodes (Iowa's state rock) form?

8

nounced *lows*) Hills, which extend from Sioux City past the Missouri border, were formed by loess—fine, gray soil left by the glaciers. Over the years, wind blew the loess into gentle hills. These unusual mounds are found only in Iowa and in some areas of China. The Sioux tribe thought they were sacred.

Young Drift Plains

Just as they did in southern and northwestern Iowa, glaciers also moved across northern and central Iowa and flattened the land. When the glaciers melted, they left behind drift, or fine layers of rocks and soil. This land is now some of the best farmland in the world. The glaciers also carved many pits into the flat ground. These holes in northern Iowa later filled with water and became lakes.

The Driftless Area

One part of northeastern Iowa did not experience the glaciers' deep-freeze. This area near the Mississippi River is nicknamed the Switzerland of Iowa because, like the mountainous European country of Switzerland, it has many hills, valleys, and ridges.

The shapes of the Loess Hills are affected by rainfall and flooding, which remove loess from the hills.

9

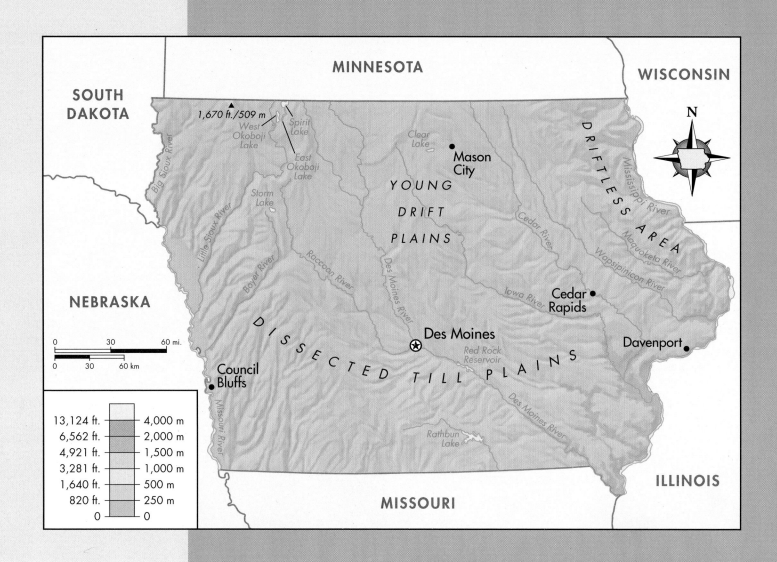

SOUTH DAKOTA

MINNESOTA

WISCONSIN

N

1,670 ft./509 m

West Okoboji Lake

Spirit Lake

East Okoboji Lake

Clear Lake

Mason City

YOUNG DRIFT PLAINS

DRIFTLESS AREA

Big Sioux River

Little Sioux River

Storm Lake

Raccoon River

Boyer River

Des Moines River

Cedar River

Iowa River

Mississippi River

Maquoketa River

Wapsipinicon River

NEBRASKA

0   30   60 mi.

0   30   60 km

DISSECTED   TILL   PLAINS

Des Moines

Cedar Rapids

Davenport

Red Rock Reservoir

Council Bluffs

Missouri River

Des Moines River

Rathbun Lake

ILLINOIS

13,124 ft.	4,000 m
6,562 ft.	2,000 m
4,921 ft.	1,500 m
3,281 ft.	1,000 m
1,640 ft.	500 m
820 ft.	250 m
0	0

MISSOURI

It is also called the Driftless Area, since the wind and rain carried away most of the area's drift. While the soil may be too poor for farming, this pretty corner of the state is a favorite place for hiking and canoeing.

FERTILE FARMLAND

Thanks to the till, drift, and a good climate, almost all of Iowa is used as farmland. Famous American poet Robert Frost thought that Iowa's rich, dark land looked "good enough to eat without putting it through vegetables." Iowa is home to about 95,000 farms and about one quarter of the country's best soil.

Iowa soil is rich, dark, and extremely fertile.

Located in northwestern Iowa, Kalsow Prairie State Preserve is one of the few remaining prairies in the state.

Unfortunately, years of rain have washed away much of the original 24 inches (61 centimeters) of topsoil to less than 8 inches (20 cm) in some parts of the state. This soil loss is called erosion. Farmers work hard to conserve the soil. They dig ditches to help water drain properly. They also plant crops on tiles of land that look like a patchwork quilt. This helps the land to drain without losing the soil.

The flat, gently sloping, grass-covered prairie used to cover a good portion of Iowa. At one time, the prairie grass grew as high as 6 feet (1.8 m). The early settlers called it a "sea of grass." Today, only a small bit of the original prairie remains.

PLANTS AND ANIMALS

Many kinds of wildflowers give Iowa's landscape patches of color. Asters, shooting-stars, and purple avens stand out brightly against patches of tall, sandy prairie grass and emerald hills. Perhaps the prettiest and sweetest-smelling Iowa wildflower is the wild rose, the state flower.

Iowa's state tree is the oak tree. Birches, maples, and hickory trees also grow in the Hawkeye State. Iowa is especially beautiful in autumn, when the trees change colors.

Many animals roam Iowa's landscape, including coyotes, raccoons, mink, muskrats, foxes, and white-tailed deer. Many game birds also nest in the state, including ring-necked pheasants, partridges, turkeys, and quail. Eagles, cardinals, blue jays, and the state bird—the goldfinch—live in Iowa all year long. Orioles, bluebirds, Canada geese, and scarlet tanagers fly through Iowa seasonally.

Ring-necked pheasants are found throughout Iowa.

FIND OUT MORE

Iowa is home to many kinds of plants, animals, fish, and birds. With so much wildlife, why should it matter to Iowans if some of these plants and animals become extinct, or die off? What are some things people can do to help keep these living things safe?

RIVERS AND LAKES

Iowa has a unique natural "fence." The Mississippi and Missouri Rivers—the longest and second-longest rivers in the country—carve out the state's eastern and western boundaries. Iowa is the only state bordered by two rivers. For the most part, Iowa's eastern rivers, including the Rock River, flow into the Mississippi River. The state's western rivers, such as the Boyer and Little Sioux Rivers, join the Missouri River.

One of Iowa's longest rivers is the Des Moines. It flows southeasterly for about 525 miles (845 km) until it joins the Mississippi near the state's southeast border with Illinois and Missouri. The Mississippi has many locks and dams in Iowa to raise and lower boats and barges so they can easily make their way down the river.

Flowing for 329 miles (529 km), the Iowa River begins in the north and makes its way southeast. It flows into the Mississippi below Muscatine. This river is equipped with a flood control system to keep it from overflowing its banks during rainy spells.

Thanks to the glaciers, northern Iowa now boasts its own version of the Great Lakes (the Great Lakes are five connecting lakes in North America that make up the world's largest body of fresh water). Spirit Lake, Storm Lake, Clear Lake, and West and East Okoboji Lakes are all

Lake Okoboji is one of the best recreational spots in Iowa.

EXTRA! EXTRA!

Sandhill cranes live in Iowa and other midwestern states during summer, but they prefer spending the winters in sunny Florida. On their trip south, these gray birds fly up to 300 miles (483 km) each day.

popular resort areas in Iowa. People love to fish, boat, and swim in their crystal blue water. Several man-made lakes, such as the Coralville Reservoir on the Iowa River and Red Rock Reservoir on the Des Moines, give Iowans plenty of water to drink.

CLIMATE

Iowans experience many kinds of weather. Iowa winters can get very cold. Most winter days, temperatures range from 14° to 24° Fahrenheit (–10 to –4° Celsius). The coldest temperature ever recorded in Iowa was an icy –47°F (–44°C) at Washta in 1912 and in Elkader in 1996.

Summer weather is hot and humid (moist). The temperature usually reaches about 85°F (29°C), but the humidity makes it feel much hotter. While people may not enjoy this muggy weather, the state's long, hot

FIND OUT MORE

Tornadoes are dangerous forces of nature. What causes a tornado? How can you keep safe during a tornado?

A tornado touched down in Dunkerton on May 11, 2000. About 10 people were injured.

summers are perfect for raising soybeans, corn, oats, and wheat. Iowa's warmest temperature was 117°F (47°C) at Atlantic and at Logan in 1936.

Temperatures can dip 50 degrees in one day, so Iowans keep their sweaters handy, even during warm months. These dramatic changes usually happen when warm air from the Gulf of Mexico meets with cold air from the Pacific or Arctic Oceans. Sometimes these quick changes in temperature cause dangerous tornadoes,

called "twisters." These funnel-like columns of air often occur during thunderstorms and cause a great deal of damage. Iowans see about 30 twisters each year. The state is considered part of "Tornado Alley," a section of the midwestern United States that receives more than its share of twisters.

Thunderstorms are common in spring and summer, when most of Iowa averages 31 inches (79 cm) of rainfall. In winter, huge snowstorms called blizzards may dump up to 3 feet (.9 m) of snow on the state. This blanket of snow usually covers most of Iowa from December to March. The wind makes the snow drift. In northern Iowa, snowdrifts sometimes grow so tall that they hide cars and tractors. Besides contributing to the state's drinking water supply, all this snow helps keep the soil moist and ready for spring planting.

Iowa winters can be harsh, with plenty of snow.

Too much rain can cause flooding in such a flat region. After heavy rains in 1993, Des Moines residents stacked 1.5 million sandbags along the banks of the Des Moines and Raccoon Rivers to hold back rising waters. Farther east, residents of Dubuque and Davenport battled the swelling waters of the Mississippi River. The rivers eventually overflowed and caused terrible damage to crops and property.

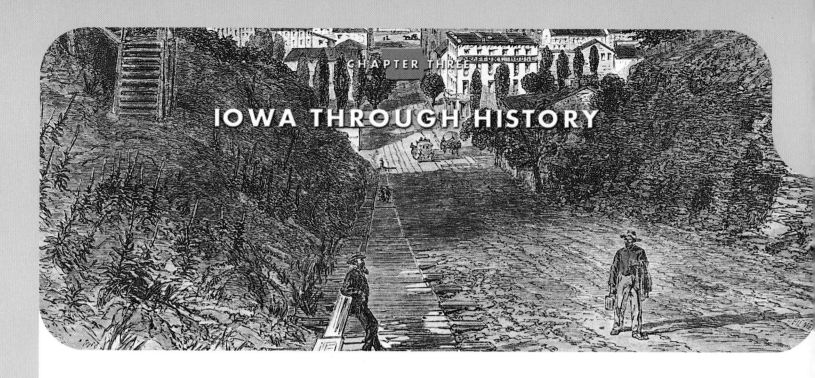

CHAPTER THREE

IOWA THROUGH HISTORY

About 13,000 years ago, after the last of the glaciers melted, early Native Americans called Paleo-Indians lived in the area that is today called Iowa. They roamed across the land and hunted large, prehistoric creatures such as mammoth and mastodon.

Centuries later, from 500 B.C. to about A.D. 1000, the Woodland people lived in small villages in present-day Iowa. They ate squash and corn that they grew on the fertile land. The Woodland people were also talented potters. They took clay from the earth and shaped it into pots and bowls, then baked them until they became hard. The Woodland people traded their ceramics with other early Native American tribes who lived as far west as the Rocky Mountains.

The Woodland people's most amazing trademarks are the mounds they built from dirt and stones. These people are sometimes called the Mound Builders. They created these burial mounds, which were

This drawing shows a view of Dubuque in 1873.

designed in the shapes of birds, bears, and other animals, to honor their dead. From an airplane, you can still clearly see the largest tomb near Clayton. The 135-foot (41-m) long Great Woman Mound is shaped like a giant woman. These Effigy Mounds, as they are named, are now preserved as a national monument. They are located along the Mississippi River in northeastern Iowa, where 196 mounds dot the countryside.

Hundreds of years later, descendants of these early people settled in Iowa. Various Native American groups such as the Iowa, Illinois, Miami, Ottawa, and Sioux settled near the Mississippi River. The Oneota built villages across the state. They hunted bison, elk, and deer. They also raised corn, beans, and pumpkins in the rich soil and gathered nuts, berries, and other plants. The Omaha, Oto, and Missouri hunted buffalo in the western part of the state.

EARLY EXPLORATION

The first Europeans to explore Iowa were French explorers Louis Joliet and Jacques Marquette. In 1673, Joliet, a fur trader and mapmaker from Canada, and Marquette, a French missionary, explored the area along the Mississippi River. During their journey, they boated through present-day Iowa and were the first Europeans to arrive in the state. In 1682, French explorer René-Robert Cavelier, Sieur de La Salle explored the Mississippi River Valley. He named this large piece of land Louisiana,

after his king, Louis XIV, and claimed it for France. It later became known as the Louisiana Territory.

Many fur-bearing animals, such as deer, otter, bear, marmot, fox, and beaver, lived in this area, and the Native Americans hunted and trapped them. They used the pelts (furs) to make fur hats to keep them

Louis Joliet and Father Jacques Marquette explored along the Mississippi River.

warm during cold winters. Soon, Canadians and Europeans began offering rifles and other manufactured goods to Native Americans in exchange for these pelts.

Fur trading became an important industry in the New World. Not many fur-bearing animals could be found in Europe. Since the weather in Europe was often cold, there was a large demand for warm fur coats and fashionable clothing. To help fill this demand, some Canadian trappers set up trading posts along the Mississippi River. The town of Keokuk was one of these trading centers. The city of Bellevue also grew around a fur-trading post.

Other than fur traders, few Europeans visited Iowa during the next century. In 1788, French-Canadian Julien Dubuque became Iowa's first European settler. He became friends with the area's Native Americans and later married the daughter of the Mesquaki leader. The Fox people also gave Dubuque permission to mine lead on their land.

The city of Dubuque is named after Julien Dubuque, the first European settler in Iowa.

THE LOUISIANA PURCHASE

On April 30, 1803, France sold its Louisiana Territory to the United States for $15 million. This sale is called the Louisiana Purchase. The 800,000 square mile (2 million sq km) plot of land reached from the

Mississippi River to the Rocky Mountains. The Louisiana Territory was so large that it doubled the size of the United States. Since it cost only four cents per acre, the purchase was a bargain. Present-day Iowa (part of the Louisiana territory) was now officially part of the United States.

President Thomas Jefferson hoped to find a water route across the new territory to the Pacific Ocean. In 1804 he asked Meriwether Lewis, his private secretary and former soldier, and Lewis's friend, William Clark, to travel west of the Mississippi River in search of this route. On their way, Lewis and Clark passed by western Iowa. The trip was difficult. One member of their team, Sergeant Charles Floyd, died as they traveled up the Missouri River. His friends buried him near Sioux City.

William Clark wrote some colorful descriptions of the area. (Words are spelled in a way that was common in his time.) "The plains of this countrey are covered with a leek green grass. . . groops of shrubs covered with the most delecious froot is to be seen in every direction, and nature appears to have exerted herself to butify the senery by the variety of flours. . . which strikes and profumes the sensation."

During their expedition, Lewis and Clark kept a diary in which they drew pictures and wrote descriptions of the things they saw.

After hearing about the fertile landscape, pioneers from the east became interested in the area. Many people traveled there and started farms. As more and more settlers arrived, however, more land was needed. Many Native Americans living in the area were forced out to make room for more white settlers. In 1804, the American government forced the Sauk to give up their land in the neighboring state of Illinois. During the next thirty years, many members of the Sauk peacefully moved across the river to Iowa.

The Black Hawk War was devastating for the Fox and Sauk.

Although most of the Native Americans were friendly, the United States government did not take chances. To protect the settlers, they built Iowa's first army outpost, Fort Madison, on the upper Mississippi River in 1808. The army stopped using the fort as a military base in 1813. In the 1830s, more settlers moved to this area, which developed into a town. They named the town Fort Madison, for the former army outpost.

Some of the Sauk were unhappy about their move to Iowa. Black Hawk, a Sauk leader, was angry that the United States had cheated his people. In 1832, Black Hawk led a group of Fox and Sauk into Illinois, but the United States Army drove them back across the Mississippi River. War broke out between both sides. This is known as the Black Hawk War. Many Native Americans were killed as a result of the war.

To punish the Sauk, the Army took over an additional 50 miles (80 km) of their land. This was called the Black Hawk Purchase, even though it was not a purchase at all. Although Black Hawk had lost his land, the chief left an important mark on Iowa.

STATEHOOD

Word of the area's rich farmland and wide-open spaces spread quickly. Soon, many more European settlers moved to the region hoping to build houses and start farms. One of these pioneers, Albert Lea, officially named the territory Iowa after the Iowa tribe.

Present-day Iowa was originally part of the Missouri Territory, which was set up in 1812. Later it became part of Michigan Territory, and then part of the huge Wisconsin Territory.

In 1838, Iowa had enough people to become a separate territory, called the Iowa territory. Iowa's original territory was only about half the size of the present-day state.

President James Polk declared Iowa a state in 1846.

The city of Burlington served as its capital. One year later, Iowa City replaced Burlington as the capital.

In 1844, Congress voted to allow Iowa to become a state. However, Iowans voted against statehood because they thought the proposed state was too small. A few years later, the government finally agreed to extend Iowa's western border to the Missouri River. In 1846, President James Polk signed the document that officially created the country's twenty-ninth state. At the time, Iowa was home to almost 200,000 people. Des Moines replaced Iowa City as the capital in 1857 because Des Moines was located in the center of the state.

A GROWING STATE

As the state developed, settlers continued to buy land from the Native Americans. Like the Sauk, these tribes were not happy about giving up their land. When the Mesquaki realized they had made a mistake by selling their territory, they decided to play the white man's game. In 1857, the Mesquaki won one of few Native American victories. They convinced the Iowa government to let them buy back 80 acres

(32 hectares) of land in east-central Iowa. The Mesquaki still own this land today.

Unlike the Mesquaki, the Sioux made their own rules. In 1857, some Sioux became angry because white pioneers had settled along Spirit Lake. The Sioux considered this area holy. In 1857, the Sioux killed more than 35 pioneers and captured several others living in the area. This incident is known as the Spirit Lake Massacre.

After the Spirit Lake Massacre, the government worried that settlers would be afraid to move to the area. However, fear did not stop the pioneers who desperately wanted their own plot of land. At the time of the Black Hawk War only about 50 settlers lived in Iowa. Soon after, people from other states, including Ohio, Wisconsin, Michigan, and New York, moved to the territory, eager to claim their own plot of this beautiful countryside. Many settlers were experienced farmers. Others decided to switch jobs and give farming a try.

Pioneers paid $1.25 per acre for the land, but it was too knotted with thick grasses and roots to farm. In order to reach the 2-foot (.6-m) thick layer of topsoil under the prairie, farmers hired professional prairie breakers. These men used breaking plows—large tools pulled by oxen—to cut the soil and loosen it enough for planting.

Pioneers built houses from whatever materials they could find. In eastern Iowa, they cut down trees and built log cabins. Since few trees

Breaking the hard prairie land required several men and strong oxen.

grew in western Iowa, they made bricks from thick sod and used them to build homes. Sod houses, called soddies, stayed warm in winter and cool on hot summer days.

Farming was not the only industry in Iowa. Between 1850 and 1870, steamboats—large boats powered by steam engines—began to make their way down the Mississippi River. These boats became an important part of industry in Iowa because they could transport crops to different states. They also carried lumber into Iowa from other, more wooded states such as Wisconsin and Minnesota. Around this time, many more Iowans began building homes from logs instead of sod.

By 1870, almost 1.2 million people lived in the Hawkeye State. Many were immigrants (people who had moved there from other countries). Among them, Dutch, Irish, English, Scandinavian, and German people left their home countries because of hunger or other problems. They hoped to find a better life in Iowa.

RAILROADS

Iowans knew it was important to become part of America's growing railroad network. Since the state was located in the middle of the country, trains would bring opportunities for commerce (the buying and selling of goods) and work.

In 1855, the state's first railroad was finished, but it was short. It ran between the eastern cities of Davenport and Muscatine. Iowa City wanted to quickly add a railroad

Settlers worked together to build log cabins.

FIND OUT MORE

Many immigrants from other countries moved to Iowa in search of a better life. They brought their traditions with them. From what country do your ancestors come? What language did they speak? Do you still carry on their traditions at home?

The railroad brought new people in, hauled goods out, and provided a link to the rest of the country.

line. Its people promised to reward workers if they finished the Davenport–Iowa City line by New Year's Day 1856. The workers toiled from early morning to late night and lit huge bonfires to keep warm in the icy, –20°F (–29°C) temperatures. Just before midnight on December 31, 1855, the workers hammered in the last railroad spike.

The first railroad to cross the entire state of Iowa, from the Mississippi River to Council Bluffs, was not finished until 1867. Just three years later, four railroads crossed the Hawkeye State, making it easy to transport Iowa's crops all over the country. These railroads did more

than just carry food, livestock, and supplies in and out of Iowa—they made Iowa an important economic center of the United States.

THE CIVIL WAR

Just as Iowa was growing, so was the rest of the United States. However, the economies of the northern and southern states were very different. The South did not have many cities. Most Southerners earned a living by farming. The South was known for its large cotton and tobacco farms, called plantations, that were staffed by hundreds of workers.

Many of these workers were African-American slaves. Plantation owners purchased slaves and often treated them very poorly. Slaves were not considered people, and they had no rights. Sometimes during slave auctions, slave traders heartlessly separated children from their parents. Slaves toiled from dawn until dusk, picking crops, running errands, tending to the owners' children, and working on the plantation. They often lived in poorly constructed buildings and were not given enough to eat. Many slaves were beaten.

Life in the North was different. The North had a diversified economy, which means that people worked in factories as well as agriculture. Factory workers earned wages. Most northerners thought that slavery was wrong.

Since the North and South could not agree on slavery, some states were "free states" while others were "slave states." The United States government tried to keep the two in balance. Iowa was the country's first free state west of the Mississippi. Most Iowans were against slavery. In fact, keeping slaves in Iowa was not allowed.

At the risk of going to prison, abolitionists (people who spoke out against slavery) started the Underground Railroad. It was not a real railroad; it was a system in which people helped runaway slaves escape to freedom in Canada. The railroad was made up of safe houses, or "stations." "Conductors" secretly escorted the slaves from station to station. They often hid slaves under hay bales or corn piles.

Traveling along the Underground Railroad was dangerous for slaves, who were often hunted by their owners.

The disagreement about slavery created tension between North and South. Southerners felt strongly that they should have the right to decide for themselves whether or not to own slaves, rather than be told by the government. To protect their rights, the people of South Carolina decided to secede from, or leave, the United States in 1860. Mississippi, Florida, Alabama, Georgia, Louisiana, and Texas soon followed suit. On February 4, 1861, officials from these states met in Montgomery, Alabama, and created their own constitution (a country's written laws and governing principles). They decided to unite and call themselves the Confederate States of America. The United States was now divided.

The Civil War (1861–1865) began in 1861, in part because North and South could not agree on the issue of slavery and states' rights. The Union (North), fought against the Confederacy (South). About 80,000 Iowans fought for the Union. In 1865 the Union won the war, and slavery was abolished.

As a result, African-Americans were no longer slaves—they were American citizens with rights. Still, they were not equal in the eyes of many people. Quite a few states practiced segregation up until the 1950s. Segregation was the practice of separating blacks and whites in public places,

WHO'S WHO IN IOWA?

Carrie Chapman Catt (1859–1947) graduated from the Iowa Agricultural College (now Iowa State University) in 1880, at a time when most women did not finish high school. Throughout her life, she fought for women's rights in Iowa and all over the world. She was president of the National American Woman Suffrage Association (an organization that worked for women's right to vote) and founded the League of Women Voters. In 1920, her years of hard work paid off when Congress passed a law that gave women the right to vote. Catt grew up in Charles City.

including schools. Iowa, on the other hand, opened its schools to all races from the start. In 1868, the state also gave African-American men the right to vote. President Ulysses S. Grant said that Iowa was "the nation's one bright radical star."

THE INDUSTRIAL AGE

The Civil War helped boost Iowa's economy because the state supplied the North with a good deal of food and grain. After the war, the country's economy shifted from a foundation of farming to an industrial base (factory work and manufacturing). As a result, Iowa's farms became more important than ever, because most northern workers relied on Iowa's crops. More immigrants, mostly from Germany, moved to Iowa to work in the booming farm industry.

In the 1860s, Iowa farmers began to wonder whether the railroads were a friend or an enemy. Railroad companies could charge any price they wished to carry the farmers' products to their destinations. Quite often, railroad companies charged the farmers ridiculously high prices. It wasn't long before Iowa farmers were losing money.

Farmers knew something had to be done to stop the railroads from taking all their profits. They formed a group called the Grange that was designed to stand up for farmers' rights. About 100,000 Iowa farmers joined.

In 1874, the state government passed a law and set up a commission (a group of people) to keep watch over railroad companies. Unfortu-

Grange halls often served as community centers, where people gathered for social events as well as official meetings.

nately, since many railroad employees served on this commission, Iowa's farmers did not enjoy relief until about 15 years later.

In the early 1900s, more Americans worked in industry. Fred Maytag made people's lives easier when he invented the washing machine. Factories in Newton turned out many of the modern machines. Much-needed farm tools and tractors were made in eastern Iowa. Factories in Muscatine turned freshwater mussel shells into pretty buttons. Still, Iowa continued to be an important farming state. At this time, most Iowans earned a lot of money. The people of the Hawkeye State were happy and successful.

In 1917, the United States entered into World War I (1914–1918). Private Merle Hay of Glidden was one of the first three American soldiers to give his life for his country. Hay died in France, where a statue was erected to honor his memory.

During the war, Iowa farmers fared well. They sold crops to European countries who were also fighting in the war. Dairy farming was also becoming an important part of Iowa's economy. Many farmers borrowed money from banks so they could buy more land and equipment to help them keep up with the demand.

THE GREAT DEPRESSION

When the war ended in 1918, so did the demand for Iowa's crops. Many farmers could not repay their loans. Land prices fell dramatically in the early 1920s, and many industries such as mining, railroads, and banks also began to lose money. As a result, many people lost their jobs.

Things got worse when the stock market crashed, and the Great Depression (1929–1939) began. People all over the United States lost money on their business investments, and many couldn't afford to buy food or keep

WHO'S WHO IN IOWA?

Herbert Hoover (1874–1964) was elected the thirty-first president of the United States in 1928. In 1929, the stock market crashed and America's economy failed. Many Americans blamed Hoover for the country's problems. In 1932, Hoover lost his presidential seat to Franklin Delano Roosevelt. Hoover was born in West Branch.

their homes. Crop prices fell even lower, and many more workers lost their jobs. To keep their families from starving, some farmers sold their corn for only 10 cents a bushel—less than their ancestors had charged in 1857.

In 1932, more problems arose for farmers. To prevent children from contracting tuberculosis, a contagious disease of the lungs, Iowa's government wanted to test dairy cattle for infected milk. Already down on their luck because of the hardships of the Great Depression, dairy farmers in Cedar and Muscatine Counties said they would shoot any veterinarian who came to test their cows. Governor Dan Turner sympathized

FIND OUT MORE

Tuberculosis can kill humans if it is not treated quickly. How does a doctor know if someone has tuberculosis? How can you avoid getting this disease?

with the farmers, but said the cattle had to be tested. He believed that children's safety came first. United States Army troops helped keep peace during these tests. This incident became known as the Cow War.

The Great Depression was a difficult decade for most Americans. In an effort to boost the economy, President Franklin D. Roosevelt created the National Recovery Administration, a group that made sure workers were paid fairly and that all industries could fairly compete with one another. Roosevelt also started the Civilian Conservation Corps, an organization that gave people jobs planting forests and drying out swamplands. Jobs like these helped many Iowans to get back on their feet.

FIND OUT MORE

Electricity makes everyone's life easier. Even so, Iowa's Amish people choose to live without modern conveniences such as cars, electricity, and telephones. They live much like Iowa's early settlers. Instead of driving cars and gas-powered tractors, for example, they use horse-drawn carriages and farm equipment. Instead of electric lamps, they use candles and lanterns. What new tasks you would have to learn if you did not have electricity? Find out how the Amish live without it.

Iowans' lives also changed for the better with the wider use of electricity. Life on the farm improved thanks to radios, household appliances, and farming equipment. Chores such as washing, plowing, and cooking became easier. Thanks to televisions and telephones, farmers and country dwellers no longer felt isolated.

In 1941, America entered World War II (1939–1945). Many Iowans served in the armed forces during the war, including five brothers, the Sullivans, from Waterloo. They signed up to serve in the Navy, and together they were assigned to duty on the U.S.S. *Juneau*. In November 1942, the ship was sunk off the coast of Guadalcanal, and all five young men lost their lives. This tragedy changed the military's rules. Since then, brothers are not permitted to serve on the same ship.

Although many lives were lost during the war, it helped pull the United States out of the Depression. Many American industries, such as the manufacturing of metal and farm equipment, thrived throughout the 1940s. As a result, Iowa farmers got a much-needed boost. They helped feed the country during this trying period.

New farming machinery such as speedier stalk cutters, planters, cultivators, and harvesters, made it easier than ever to plant and harvest crops. However, because these newly invented machines cut down on the number of farm employees, many rural people were out of jobs.

The five Sullivan brothers—Albert, Madison, Joseph, Francis, and George—served on the same Navy ship during World War II.

The names of many places in Iowa have interesting origins.

Name	Comes From or Means
Des Moines	French phrase "la Rivière des Moines," or the river of monks
Dubuque	Named for Julien Dubuque, a French miner who settled the town in 1788
Muscatine	Named for the Mascoutine tribe
Oskaloosa	Named for the wife of a Seminole leader named Osceole; it means "last of the beautiful"
Ottumwa	Native American word meaning "rippling waters"
Winterset	The town's original residents wanted to call their town Somerset or Summerset; on a cold day, someone suggested Winterset instead

Throughout the 1960s, more Iowans moved to cities such as Cedar Rapids and Des Moines to find different work. According to the 1960 census, more Iowans lived in cities than in the country for the first time in history. As a result, Iowa had to change its laws in 1965 to make sure that the cities had enough leaders in state government.

When Iowans moved to the cities, the state's economy shifted from agricultural to industrial-agricultural. More people worked in city factories. Although they were far from their farms, most people held jobs in food processing and farm equipment manufacturing industries to stay close to their farming roots.

RECENT TIMES

In the late 1970s and early 1980s, crop prices rose. Although Iowa farmers were earning more money than ever before, hard times were not yet over. The cost of farming equipment, land, and supplies rose sharply. Since there was a worldwide surplus (abundance) of food, crop prices did not rise to make up the difference. Farmers once again lost money.

Many farmers had to take part-time jobs to help make ends meet. Others had to borrow money from banks to make up for their losses. By 1984, 1 in every 3 Iowa farmers had serious money problems. Not surprisingly, many young people left the state to find work. With few people making money and so many leaving, Iowa's economy was in danger of collapsing, just as the country's economy had done during the Great Depression.

Iowa's leaders helped to find new opportunities for workers. Computers were becoming an increasingly important part of everyday life, and more Iowa businesses began to invest in technology. Several technology companies opened offices in the state. As a result, more Iowans began to work in this field.

This industry is still growing. The Iowa Department of Economic Development and Iowa State University created a new technology partnership. Their goal is to create more technology-based businesses in the state. The government also allowed gambling in the state in the 1990s.

Many Iowans work at companies such as John Deere, a major producer of agricultural equipment.

These two industries created more jobs and brought more residents and visitors into Iowa.

Iowans still faced struggles, however. In 1993 after very heavy rains fell across the Midwest, the Mississippi River and its smaller streams and rivers flooded their banks. The flood caused millions of dollars worth of property and crop damage. Des Moines suffered the worst damage. President Bill Clinton declared the state a disaster area.

In the true spirit of Chief Black Hawk, Iowans have not given up. They have always worked to solve their problems. Today, the state's economy is growing, thanks in part to many hardworking immigrants who are moving into the state. Many new businesses have opened, and the Hawkeye State's future is looking brighter than ever.

On July 13, 1993, residents of central Iowa piled up sandbags in an effort to fight back flood waters.

CHAPTER FOUR

GOVERNING IOWA

Iowa's state motto, "Our liberties we prize and our rights we will maintain," shows how important civil rights (the right to personal freedoms) are to the people of Iowa. In 1846, Iowans spelled out their rights by writing a constitution. Iowa's constitution is a document that states the rights of its citizens. It also determines how the state will be governed. The Iowa constitution was rewritten in 1857; that version is still used today.

Iowa's government is organized like the United States government. Power is divided among three parts, called branches—the legislative branch, the executive branch, and the judicial branch.

The Iowa state capitol was built between 1871 and 1886.

LEGISLATIVE BRANCH

The legislative branch makes laws for Iowa. Members of the legislative branch create laws such as how much a person can be taxed, or how long

Members of the house of representatives meet inside the state capitol.

children must go to school. The members of the legislative branch are chosen by the people of Iowa.

Iowa's lawmaking group is called the General Assembly. The General Assembly meets every January to make new laws or to change current laws. It has two departments called houses—the senate and the house of representatives. The senate has 50 members, one from each district in Iowa. The house of representatives has 100 members. Senators serve four-year terms, and representatives are chosen every two years.

EXECUTIVE BRANCH

The executive branch carries out and enforces the laws. Iowa's governor is the head of the executive branch. The governor serves a four-year term.

The governor runs 22 departments, including public health and education. He or she has the power to veto (reject) a law that is proposed by the legislature, but the General Assembly may decide to overturn (reverse) the governor's veto. The governor also suggests how the state's money should be spent. The legislature approves his or her recommendations.

IOWA GOVERNMENT

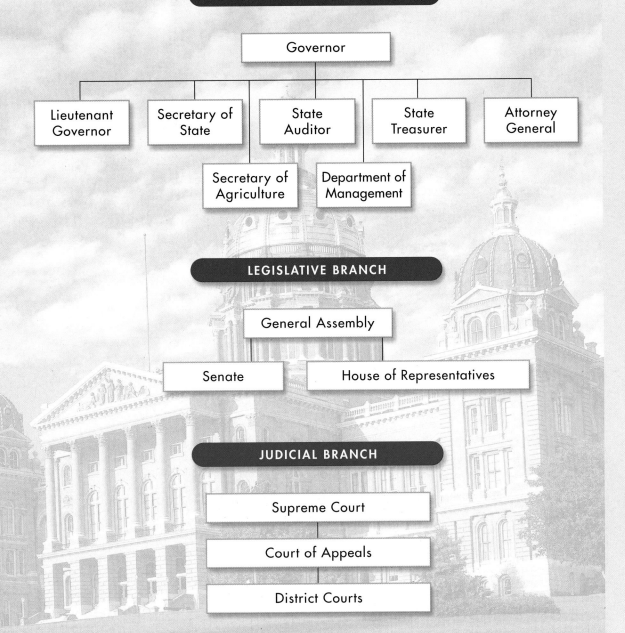

EXECUTIVE BRANCH

Governor

Lieutenant Governor

Secretary of State

State Auditor

State Treasurer

Attorney General

Secretary of Agriculture

Department of Management

LEGISLATIVE BRANCH

General Assembly

Senate

House of Representatives

JUDICIAL BRANCH

Supreme Court

Court of Appeals

District Courts

Other members of the executive branch help the governor. The lieutenant governor is elected along with the governor. If anything should happen that would prevent the governor from serving, the lieutenant governor steps in and runs the state. The governor decides what the lieutenant governor's duties will be.

Each year, the auditor examines the records of every department in Iowa. This officer checks the finances of every local governmental body that receives money from the state, including counties, cities, and school districts. The treasurer keeps track of the state's money, or treasury. The secretary of agriculture is a particularly important position in Iowa. This official oversees all farming matters within the Hawkeye State. This person also promotes and improves laws that relate to farmers and farming businesses in Iowa.

JUDICIAL BRANCH

The judicial branch interprets the laws and resolves disagreements relating to the law. It is made up of judges and courts. Each year, about one million cases are tried in Iowa courts. To help the judicial process run smoothly, the state has several kinds of courts for different cases.

Many cases begin in district courts. District courts handle two kinds of cases. Criminal cases are those in which someone has been arrested for committing a crime such as assault or armed robbery. Civil cases usually involve disputes, or disagreements, between two parties with regard to a particular law. Civil cases might include divorce hearings, adoptions, or other cases that involve children.

IOWA GOVERNORS

Name	Term	Name	Term
Ansel Briggs	1846–1850	George W. Clarke	1913–1917
Stephen P. Hempstead	1850–1854	William L. Harding	1917–1921
James W. Grimes	1854–1858	N. E. Kendell	1921–1925
Ralph P. Lowe	1858–1860	John Hammill	1925–1931
Samuel J. Kirkwood	1860–1864	Daniel W. Turner	1931–1933
William M. Stone	1864–1868	Clyde L. Herring	1933–1937
Samuel Merrill	1868–1872	Nelson G. Kraschel	1937–1939
Cyrus C. Carpenter	1872–1876	George A. Wilson	1939–1943
Samuel J. Kirkwood	1876–1877	Bourke B. Hickenlooper	1943–1945
Joshua G. Newbold	1877–1878	Robert D. Blue	1945–1949
John H. Gear	1878–1882	William S. Beardsley	1949–1954
Buren R. Sherman	1882–1886	Leo Elthon	1954–1955
William Larrabee	1886–1890	Leo A. Hoegh	1955–1957
Horace Boles	1890–1894	Herschel C. Loveless	1957–1961
Frank D. Jackson	1894–1896	Norman A. Erbe	1961–1963
Francis M. Drake	1896–1898	Harold E. Hughes	1963–1969
Leslie M. Shaw	1898–1902	Robert D. Fulton	1969
Albert B. Cummins	1902–1908	Robert Ray	1969–1983
Warren Garst	1908–1909	Terry E. Branstad	1983–1999
Beryl F. Carroll	1909–1913	Thomas J. Vilsack	1999–

If a person is not satisfied with the court's decision, he or she may appeal a judge's decision, or take their case to a higher (more important) court. This court is called the court of appeals. Iowa's state court of appeals decides if a case needs to be retried.

Located in Des Moines, the supreme court is Iowa's highest court. It has the final say on all rules of court procedure. It is also the last place in Iowa where appeals can be made. Eight justices (judges) serve on the supreme court. The justices vote for one of their members to become chief justice.

Minor cases, such as those involving traffic violations, are presented to a county magistrate, another type of judge. County magistrates also rule on cases that involve small amounts of money or property.

George W. Bush attended a pancake breakfast in Des Moines during the 2000 presidential election.

IOWA CAUCUSES

Iowa plays an important role in the United States presidential elections. Before a new president is elected, the members of all political parties (i.e. Republican, Democrat) must decide on a candidate, a person who will represent their party in the presidential race. Each party votes for its representative in small meetings called caucuses. The person who wins the most caucus votes is the state's "winner."

The Iowa Caucuses are always first in the nation. As a result, people generally feel that the Iowa caucuses give them a "sneak preview" of what will happen during the rest of the election. Today, many Americans watch the results of the Iowa Caucuses on television.

EXTRA! EXTRA!

Although they began in 1846, the Iowa Caucuses did not become popular until 1976, when the Democrats named Jimmy Carter as their presidential candidate. Carter is the only nonincumbent candidate (a candidate who was not already president) to win the Iowa Caucuses and then the presidency.

This photo shows a view of Grand Avenue in Des Moines.

TAKE A TOUR OF DES MOINES, THE STATE CAPITAL

Des Moines is located in south central Iowa, where the Des Moines and Raccoon Rivers meet. According to the 2000 census, 198,682 people live there, making Des Moines Iowa's largest city. It is a fairly large community, covering 67 square miles (174 sq km). Des Moines is an interesting blend of historic and modern-day culture.

One of the first things people notice when they come to the city is the gleaming top of the capitol building. This 275-foot (84-m) high dome is covered with 23-karat gold leaf and sparkles in the sun. A lantern

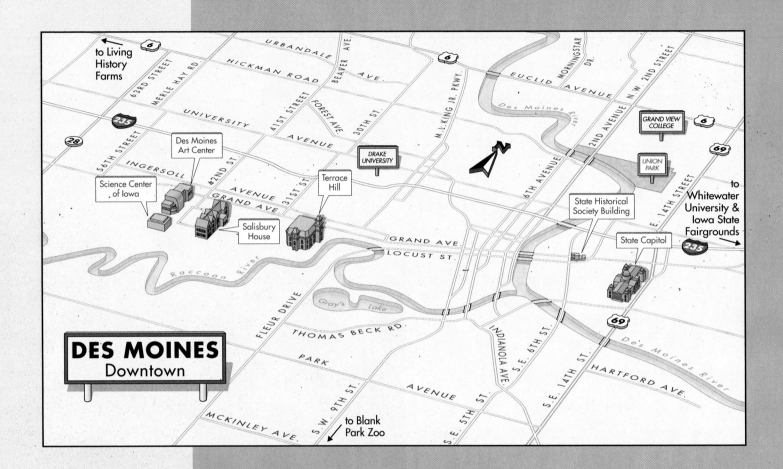

to Living
History
Farms

URBANDALE

to
Whitewater
University &
Iowa State
Fairgrounds

DES MOINES
Downtown

to Blank
Park Zoo

GRAND VIEW
COLLEGE

UNION
PARK

DRAKE
UNIVERSITY

Des Moines Art Center

Science Center of Iowa

Terrace Hill

Salisbury House

State Historical Society Building

State Capitol

HICKMAN ROAD

BEAVER AVE.

EUCLID AVENUE

MORNINGSTAR DR.

2ND AVENUE N.W.

2ND STREET

63RD STREET

MERLE HAY RD.

UNIVERSITY AVENUE

41ST STREET

FOREST AVE.

30TH ST.

M. L. KING JR. PKWY.

Des Moines River

6TH AVENUE

E. 14TH STREET

56TH STREET

INGERSOLL AVENUE

42ND ST.

31ST ST.

GRAND AVE.

GRAND AVE.

LOCUST ST.

Raccoon River

FLEUR DRIVE

Gray's Lake

THOMAS BECK RD.

PARK AVENUE

S.W. 9TH ST.

MCKINLEY AVE.

S.W. 5TH ST.

INDIANOLA AVE.

S.E. 6TH ST.

S.E. 14TH ST.

HARTFORD AVE.

Des Moines River

decorates the top. Inside the capitol, the law library has a four-story circular staircase. Its ceilings are decorated with large paintings called murals, and the rest of the building features carved wood railings and mosaics (pictures made from tiny pieces of tile). Some senators and representatives have offices inside the capitol, and they meet as a group in the legislative chambers to decide upon laws.

Iowa's first capitol building was located in Iowa City. In 1857, the Old Brick Capitol in Des Moines became the state's center of government. It served as the capitol for 26 years before being destroyed by fire in 1892. The Soldier's and Sailor's Monument, in memory of those who served in the Civil War, now stands in place of the Old Brick Capitol.

Des Moines is home to more than just the state government. Sports fans enjoy cheering the city's teams on to victory, including the AAA baseball team, the Iowa Cubs; its professional hockey team, the Des Moines Buckaneers; and its professional soccer team, the Des Moines Menace. Aside from sports, the city also offers much to do in the way of music, art, dance, and theater.

A mosaic on the second floor of the capitol, called "Westward," shows early settlers coming into Iowa by wagon.

EXTRA! EXTRA!

Des Moines was founded in 1843. The city's original name was Fort Raccoon, but the United States War Department later changed the name to Fort Des Moines. This name comes from the French settlers' name for the Raccoon River, La Rivière des Moines, or "the river of monks."

The governor lives in a large mansion called Terrace Hill. It was built by millionaire Benjamin Franklin Allen in 1869, but it did not become the governor's mansion until 1971. Visitors can tour the first two floors of the home. The governor and his family live on the third floor.

Not far from the capitol is the Des Moines Art Center. This unique, modern building was designed by famous architects Eliel Saarinen, I. M. Pei, and Richard Meier. Its curving walls and balconies mimic, or copy, the curves in nature. Inside, you can see works by contemporary artists, as well as a large permanent collection of works by 19th and 20th century artists.

The Des Moines Art Center is a world-class art museum in the heart of the Midwest.

Children especially like visiting the city's Living History Farms. You can learn what life was like on a farm in 1900 by churning butter, combing wool, and making apple butter. The farms are also home to an imaginary town called Walnut Hill. This town is trapped in the year 1857. Visitors can tour its blacksmith shop, bank, schoolhouse, and general store.

Des Moines is home to two institutions of higher education—Drake University and Grand View College. Des Moines Community College is also located in the city. Other colleges in Des Moines include Hamilton Business College, the American Institute of Business, Vatterott, and the Des Moines College of Medicine.

You cannot earn a degree at Whitewater University, but you can certainly have fun there. This water park features giant water slides, wave machines, and tubing. It is a favorite way for both young and old to cool off during the hot summer months.

Each April, Drake University hosts the Drake Relays, a prestigious track and field competition.

CHAPTER FIVE

THE PEOPLE AND PLACES OF IOWA

Iowans are friendly people who look out for one another.

Most books say Iowa's farmland is its greatest resource. While farming is certainly important, Iowans would probably say its people are the state's greatest treasure. People from many different backgrounds live in the Hawkeye State. Their differences helped shape the state's unique customs and traditions.

MEET THE PEOPLE

According to the 2000 census, 2,926,324 people live in Iowa. Iowans live on farms, in small towns, and in large cities. Lately, many people have been leaving the state's farms and small towns to find better jobs and more excitement in Iowa's cities.

About 94 of every 100 Iowans come from a European background. This is not surprising. During the 1840s, pioneers and farmers from

European countries such as Ireland, Scotland, Germany, Scandinavia, Holland, and the former Czechoslovakia (now the Czech Republic and the Slovak Republic) moved to Iowa to take up farming.

Many Iowa towns celebrate their European heritage. Decorah's Vesterheim (vest-er-highm) or "western home" Museum showcases the town's Norwegian roots. Each spring, Pella becomes a Dutch wonderland. A rainbow of tulips blossom, and people wear wooden clogs and historic Dutch costumes. Many people in Elk Horn have a Danish background and speak Danish. The town's centerpiece is a large windmill that came from Denmark in 30,000 numbered pieces. It was put together like a puzzle.

A Dutch family celebrates their heritage at the Orange City Tulip Festival.

Before European settlers moved to Iowa in the 1800s, 20 Native American groups lived in the state. Today, only the Mesquaki still remain in the Hawkeye State, making up less than 1 percent of Iowans. Each August, many people attend the Mesquakie Indian Powwow near Tama. Children perform the Harvest of Bean Dance to thank the spirits for their bountiful crops, and tribe members share special foods, crafts, and customs with visitors.

SPECIAL LANGUAGE

Many Iowa residents have a German background. In fact, some Iowans—including the people who live in the Amana Colonies and the Amish communities—still speak German. Try saying these German words:

English	German	Pronunciation
Good morning	Guten tag	(goot-in-tahg)
Thank you	Danke	(don-kah)
How are you?	Wie geht's?	(vee-gates)
Please	Bitte	(bit-tah)

Even though most Iowans come from a European background, it is becoming a more diverse state. In 1985, only about 2.5 percent of Iowa schoolchildren were African-American, Hispanic, or Asian. As of 2000, the numbers have increased slightly. Today, about 3 in every 100 Iowans are Hispanic and 1 is Asian; about 2 in every 100 people are African-American.

Iowa is becoming more diverse in part due to the New Iowans Program. Currently, many Iowans are retiring, and a large number of young Iowans leave the state to find better jobs. Besides causing a decline in population, it also leaves a huge gap for workers to fill. People from other countries are happy to come to the Hawkeye State to take these jobs and start new lives. The New Iowans program not only helps immigrants find jobs and homes, but it also helps to boost Iowa's economy and population. Now, about 2 of every 100 Iowans are immigrants.

An estimated 22,300 legal immigrants have moved to Iowa since 1986. Among them, about 10,000 Bosnian immigrants live in the Hawkeye State. They were forced to leave their homes in Bosnia during the 1990s because their country was torn apart by war. Instead of living in constant fear and looking at bombed-out buildings, these people now live among friendly neighbors, have plenty of work, and enjoy peace of mind. About 7,000 have settled in Des Moines, where there are an abundance of jobs. Many Mexican immigrants have also left their home country to find a better life in Iowa.

WORKING IN IOWA

When you think of Iowa, you probably picture a large farm—and for good reason. In 1989, the state had one farm for every 27 people. Iowa is the nation's largest producer of corn and hogs, and is tied with Illinois as the nation's number one soybean producer. Most of Iowa's major crops—corn, hay, oats, and soybeans—grow in the fertile north central part of the state.

The Hawkeye State's economy revolves around its farms. Many of its citizens work on farms. Farming also contributes to other important Iowa industries such as companies that make and sell packaged foods like jelly, and the manufacture of farm machinery such as tractors. As a result, when Iowa's farmers do well, most other Iowans also do well.

Farming is not an easy way to make a living. Farming technology is constantly getting better, so farmers have to buy expensive new machinery to keep up. Land

Agriculture is a leading industry in Iowa, where there are more than 90,000 farms.

prices are also increasing, so it is hard for families to run their own farms. Today, many larger, mechanized farms have replaced family-run operations.

Since the northeast part of Iowa is too hilly for farming, its workers focus on dairy production and cattle and hog farming. Iowa is one of America's biggest producers of livestock. Children love to take drives with their families along Highway 71 in southwestern Iowa, near Audubon. There you can catch a glimpse of Albert the Bull, a 30-foot (9-m) high statue that serves as a reminder of Iowa's important beef industry.

Some Iowa farmers raise Jersey cows, shown here.

People enjoy corn in the form of cornmeal, breakfast cereal, and corn syrup, as well as in many recipes. The recipe below is a favorite for breakfast or a snack. Don't forget to ask an adult for help!

IOWA BANANA CORN BREAD

    1 tbsp. dry yeast
    2 tbsp. warm water
    1-1/4 cups cornmeal
    1-1/4 cups flour
    2 eggs
    1/2 cup mashed banana (use ripe bananas for
    sweeter bread)
    1/2 cup honey
    1/2 cup chopped almonds or walnuts (optional)
    2 tbsp. corn oil
    1 tsp. cinnamon
    1/4 tsp. nutmeg
    1/4 tsp. salt

1. Preheat oven to 325°F.
2. Soften yeast in warm water. (Make sure the water is not too hot, or it will kill the yeast and the bread will not rise.)
3. Mix cornmeal, flour, and yeast in a bowl. Beat eggs, banana, honey, and corn oil in another bowl. Add nuts, if desired.
4. Mix dry ingredients into moist ingredients until well blended.
5. Pour into greased 9 x 5-inch loaf pan.
6. Bake for 40–50 minutes or until golden brown on top. Eat plain or with butter, jam, or honey. Good warm or cold.

In factories throughout the state, Iowa workers also produce food products such as breakfast cereals, farm and construction equipment, radio and television equipment, and electronic parts. Iowa is also riding the technology wave. Numerous high-technology companies make software and computer parts in Iowa City, Cedar Rapids, and Des Moines. In fact, 17 software companies have their home bases in Des Moines.

Although Des Moines is surrounded by farms, it is an important business center. Because it is home to many major insurance companies including Equitable, Wells Fargo, Principal Mutual Life, and American Republic, most Des Moines residents work in the insurance industry. People in Des Moines also work in transportation, publishing (the popular magazine *Better Homes and Gardens* is published there), and manufacturing. Some of the products that come from manufacturers in this area include farm equipment machinery, leather goods, chemicals, bricks, metal products, dairy products, packed meat, and cement. Many people in Des Moines also work in hospitals, health care, and retail (shops).

The Hawkeye State is also the nation's biggest producer of gypsum, a powdery mineral used to make cement, plasterboard, and tile. Iowans also mine for limestone, sand, and gravel.

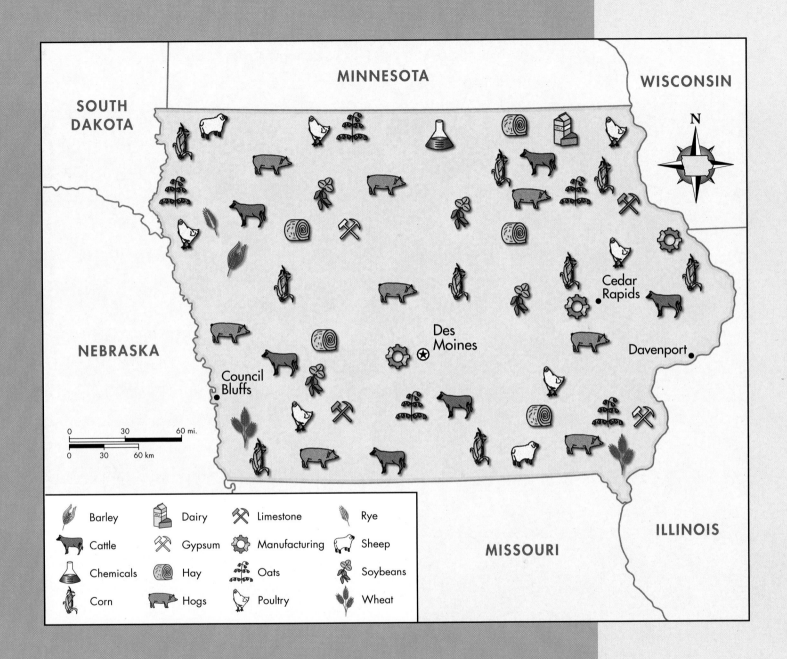

SOUTH DAKOTA

MINNESOTA

WISCONSIN

N

NEBRASKA

Cedar Rapids

Des Moines

Davenport

Council Bluffs

0 30 60 mi.

0 30 60 km

MISSOURI

ILLINOIS

	Barley		Dairy		Limestone		Rye
	Cattle		Gypsum		Manufacturing		Sheep
	Chemicals		Hay		Oats		Soybeans
	Corn		Hogs		Poultry		Wheat

More than two-thirds of Iowans work in the service industry. Those who work in this industry provide a service for people, such as health care, banking, or finance. Another growing part of the service industry is tourism. Tourism is the business of providing food, shelter, and entertainment for visitors to the state. People who work in tourism do many things. Some manage inns and restaurants. Others give tours, work at airports and train stations, and run museums and other attractions. Many people in larger cities, such as Des Moines, work in art centers and museums.

Iowa is becoming a popular place to take a vacation. In 1999, almost 19 million people visited the state. Thanks to the 1989 movie *Field of Dreams*, many people enjoy visiting the farm and baseball field in Dyersville where the movie was filmed. Robert James Waller's popular book, *The Bridges of Madison County*, also inspired vacationers to tour the covered bridges near Winterset. As a result, more Iowans in smaller towns are profiting from the tourism business. Some give tours, while

WHO'S WHO IN IOWA?

William "Buffalo Bill" Cody (1846–1917) had already delivered mail for the Pony Express, panned for gold in Colorado, and fought in the Civil War by the time he was 18 years old. Cody earned his nickname by hunting buffalo to feed the hungry workers who were building Iowa's railroads. Later, he ran a traveling show called "Buffalo Bill's Wild West." This adventure-packed spectacle included horseback stunts and mock gunfights. Today, Buffalo Bill is remembered as a legend of America's frontier days. Cody was born in Scott County.

Roseman Bridge was built in 1883. It is one of six covered bridges that remains in Madison County today.

others manage bed and breakfasts (small country inns in which guests stay overnight and are served breakfast the next morning).

TAKE A TOUR OF IOWA

Southeastern Iowa

Many people enter Iowa through the city of Davenport, near Illinois. Nestled in a loop along the Mississippi River, about 98,359 people live in this border city. A bridge connects Davenport to the neighboring Illinois towns of Moline, East Moline, and Rock Island. These cities make up what is known as the Quad Cities—the largest metropolitan area between Minneapolis, Minnesota, and St. Louis, Missouri.

Davenport was originally a Native American trading station. Today, most of Davenport looks like it did in the 1850s, complete with brick-

WHO'S WHO IN IOWA?

Grant Wood (1891–1942) was an artist who gained fame for his paintings of life in the American Midwest. The Cedar Rapids Museum of Art features America's largest collection of Wood paintings. He was born in Anamosa.

Cedar Rapids has a thriving arts community, as well as other cultural attractions.

lined streets and old-fashioned shops. Tourists and residents enjoy riding the Channel Cat Water Taxi. These open-air boats sail along the river, making stops in Iowa and Illinois.

Cedar Rapids, Iowa's second-largest city, is located northwest of Davenport. More than 120,000 people live in Cedar Rapids. Even though it started out as a single cabin, the city has grown into Iowa's most important manufacturing city and one of the state's leading artistic centers. Music lovers enjoy performances of the Cedar Rapids Symphony Orchestra and the Theatre Cedar Rapids. Through the organization's Symphony School, students can study music with the Symphony's world-famous performers.

For a long time, Cedar Rapids had America's largest percentage of residents of Czechoslovakian ancestry. Czech Village, one of the city's neighborhoods, is proud of its Eastern European heritage. Its streets are lined with ethnic shops, street markets, bakeries, and the National Czech and Slovak Museum. In fact, most of the city's Czech population keeps up a fun tradition. Just as Irish-Americans wear green or orange

on St. Patrick's Day, Czech-Americans wear red—the national color of the Czech Republic—on St. Joseph's Day, March 19.

Further south, Burlington, another border town, is the home of a very twisted landmark. Ripley's Believe It or Not declared one of the town's streets, Snake Alley, "the crookedest street in the world." This road twists and zigzags many times throughout its 275 feet (84 m).

To the west of Cedar Rapids, many people stop to visit the Amana Colonies. These seven villages were founded by a religious group called the Community of True Inspiration. The colonies' founders left Germany, where they were punished for their religious beliefs, and created the villages so they could worship freely. The people of the Amana Colonies lived communally, meaning they share the work and property equally. Many tourists visit the Amana Colonies and buy the residents' handmade furniture, clocks, and woolen products.

The Amana Colonies are a National Historic Landmark.

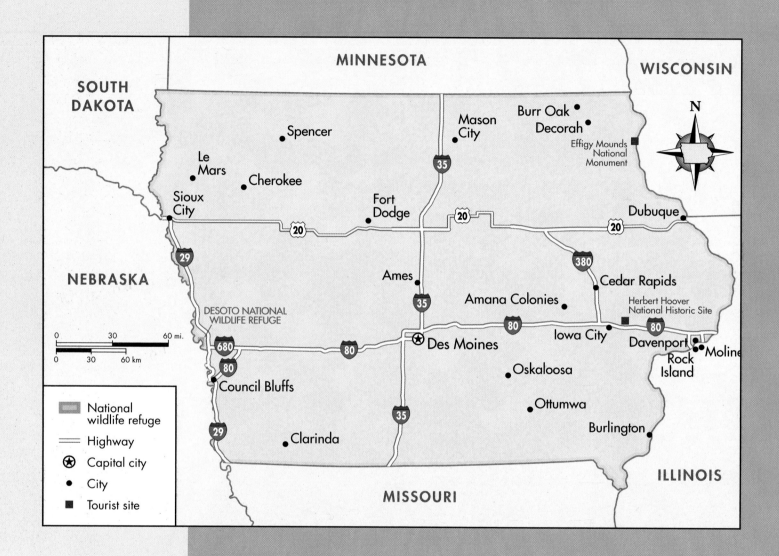

SOUTH
DAKOTA

MINNESOTA

WISCONSIN

N

Spencer

Mason
City

Burr Oak
Decorah

Effigy Mounds
National
Monument

Le
Mars

Cherokee

Sioux
City

Fort
Dodge

20

20

Dubuque

20

29

NEBRASKA

Ames

Cedar Rapids

380

DESOTO NATIONAL
WILDLIFE REFUGE

35

Amana Colonies

Herbert Hoover
National Historic Site

80

80

0   30   60 mi.

0   30   60 km

680

80

Des Moines

Iowa City

Davenport

Moline

Council Bluffs

Oskaloosa

Rock
Island

National
wildlife refuge

29

Ottumwa

Highway

Capital city

35

Burlington

City

Clarinda

Tourist site

ILLINOIS

MISSOURI

Central Iowa

Located near the state's center where the Des Moines and Raccoon Rivers meet, Des Moines is the Hawkeye State's heartbeat. Iowa's capital and largest city is home to 198,682 people. The Iowa State Fair is held each August in Des Moines. You can enjoy arm wrestling and cooking contests, livestock exhibits, and a life-sized cow made entirely from butter.

Just five miles (8 km) from the center of the state, Ames is home to Iowa State University. The university is well known for its excellent farming programs. This city of about 47,000 people also houses the Iowa Arboretum. There, nature lovers can enjoy 340 acres of gardens and trees.

Herbert Hoover was the only United States president born in Iowa, and the first president who was born west of the Mississippi River. Visitors can tour his birthplace at the Herbert Hoover Presidential Library and Museum, a national historic site, in east central Iowa at West Branch.

Southwestern Iowa

Near the Missouri River lies the small town of Clarinda. This is the birthplace of Glenn Miller, one of the country's best-known bandleaders. Visitors enjoy touring his home. In fact, each June, the town holds a Glenn Miller Festival featuring the bandleader's best-loved tunes.

In Missouri Valley, visitors can enjoy more than 8,000 acres (3,237 hectares) of wetlands, grasslands, woodland, and farmland at the

Hundreds of Canada geese take to the air at the DeSoto National Wildlife Refuge.

This photo shows a view of Sioux City from the hillside.

DeSoto Wildlife Refuge. There, you can see migrating waterfowl, especially geese and ducks. During winter, you might even catch a glimpse of the endangered bald eagle.

Northwestern Iowa

Moving northwest across the state, the Big Sioux, Floyd, and Missouri Rivers meet in Sioux City, near Iowa's border with Nebraska and South Dakota. Sioux City was settled in 1848, but the community did not receive its name until 1857. Today, it is home to 85,013 people. About 72,460 are African-American.

The city's most famous building is the Woodbury Center Courthouse. Students of the great architect Louis Sullivan built it in 1918. Its Missouri River waterfront is lined with parks where people enjoy taking walks and having picnics.

Northeast of Sioux City is the small city of Cherokee, one of the state's biggest cattle and hog-raising areas. About 6,000 people live there, and after work they enjoy the town's symphony and theater. Children especially enjoy visiting the Sanford Museum and Planetarium. There, you can get a closer look at the moon and the planets through a high-power telescope.

The down-to-earth town of Le Mars is just a few miles west of Cherokee. Because Wells Dairy is located there, the town earned the nickname "The Ice Cream Capital of the World."

Northeast Iowa

Effigy Mounds National Monument is located along the state's Upper Mississippi River Valley, just north of the small town of McGregor. There, you can see as many as 191 prehistoric mounds that the Woodland people built to honor their dead. Twenty-nine of these mounds are built to resemble bears and birds. The rest are cone-shaped or cylindrical.

A bit of sunny Italy exists in Decorah. Built in 1867, the Porter House Museum was modeled after an Italian Tuscan Villa. It is surrounded by a wall of rocks and houses an impressive collection of furnishings. Nearby, the small town of Burr Oak is where famous writer Laura Ingalls Wilder lived with her family as a child.

From prehistoric mounds to city skyscrapers, from fertile farms to offices and factories, Iowa boasts an interesting past as well as a promising future. It seems fitting that the Hawkeye State lies in the center, or the heart, of the United States. Iowa's people, industries, and cultural and artistic treasures touch the hearts of people all over the United States and the world.

WHO'S WHO IN IOWA?

Laura Ingalls Wilder (1867–1957) brought her girlhood experiences to life through a series of books called *Little House*. Amazingly, Laura did not start writing these books until she was 65. Her family's inn in Burr Oak, called the Master Hotel, is part of the Laura Ingalls Wilder Park and Museum. Every year, about 15,000 tourists visit the site.

IOWA ALMANAC

Statehood date and number: December 28, 1846/29th

State seal: The seal features a soldier standing in a wheat field, holding an American flag. He is surrounded by farm and industrial tools, with the Mississippi River in the background. Above, an eagle holds a scroll decorated with the state motto: "Our liberties we prize, and our rights we will maintain."

State flag: The flag has three vertical bars of blue, white, and red. The white section shows an eagle and the state motto, and the word *Iowa* in red.

Geographic center: Story, 5 miles (8 km) northeast of Ames

Total area/rank: 56,276 square miles (145,755 sq km)/26th

Borders: Minnesota, Wisconsin, Illinois, Missouri, Nebraska, and South Dakota

Latitude and longitude: 091.11 west; 40.55 north

Highest/lowest elevation: 1,670 feet (509 m) in Osceola County/480 feet (146 m) in Lee County

Hottest/coldest temperature: 117°F (47°C) at Atlantic and at Logan in 1936/–47°F (–44°C) at Elkader in February 1996

Land area/rank: 55,875 square miles (144,716 sq km)/23rd

Inland water area/rank: 401 square miles (1,039 sq km)/36th

Population/rank (2000 census): 2,926,324/30th

Population of major cities:

Davenport: 98,359

Des Moines: 198,682

Cedar Rapids: 120,758

Sioux City: 85,013

Origin of state name: Named for the Iowa tribe. Iowa is from the Dakota word, *Ayuhwa*, meaning "sleepy ones" or "this is the place."

State capital: Des Moines

Previous capitals: Burlington, Iowa City

Counties: 99

State government: 50 state senators, 100 state representatives

Major rivers/lakes: Boyer River, Cedar River, Nishnabotna River, Des Moines River, Floyd River, Iowa River, Little Sioux River, Maquoketa River, Mississippi River, Missouri River, Nodaway River, Skunk River, Wapsipinicon River/Clear Lake, East Okoboji Lake, Spirit Lake, Storm Lake, West Okoboji Lake, Rathburn Lake, Saylorville Lake, Red Rock Lake

Farm products: Corn, soybeans, wheat, and dairy products

Livestock: Hogs, cattle

Manufactured products: Electrical machinery, food, furniture, and electrical equipment

Mining products: Stone, gypsum, sand, shale, slate, and gravel

Fishing products: Bass, bluegill, carp, catfish, crappie, northern pike, perch, sucker, walleye

Bird: Eastern goldfinch

Fairs: Iowa State Fair, All Iowa Fair, Cattle Congress, county fairs

Flower: Wild rose

Motto: "Our liberties we prize, and our rights we will maintain."

Nickname: Hawkeye State (official), Land Where the Tall Corn Grows, the Corn State, and the Nation's Breadbasket (unofficial)

Rock: Geode

Song: "The Song of Iowa"

Tree: Oak

Wildlife: Beaver, chipmunk, coyote, deer fox, gopher, mink, muskrat, opossum, rabbit, raccoon, squirrel, skunk, white-tail deer; endangered animals: bald eagle, Indiana bat, Iowa snail, peregrine falcon, pearly mussel, piping plover, sturgeon

Birds: Blue jay, Canada goose, cardinal, duck, hawk, partridge, prairie chicken, red-winged blackbird, robin, starling, tufted titmouse

TIME**LINE**

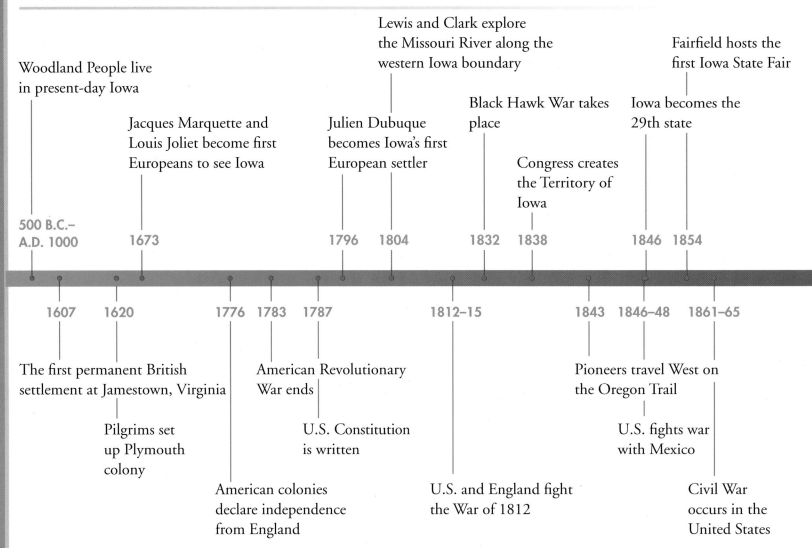

IOWA STATE **HISTORY**

Woodland People live
in present-day Iowa

Jacques Marquette and
Louis Joliet become first
Europeans to see Iowa

Lewis and Clark explore
the Missouri River along the
western Iowa boundary

Julien Dubuque
becomes Iowa's first
European settler

Black Hawk War takes
place

Congress creates
the Territory of
Iowa

Fairfield hosts the
first Iowa State Fair

Iowa becomes the
29th state

500 B.C.–
A.D. 1000   1673   1796 1804   1832 1838   1846 1854

1607 1620   1776 1783 1787   1812–15   1843 1846–48 1861–65

The first permanent British
settlement at Jamestown, Virginia

American Revolutionary
War ends

Pilgrims set
up Plymouth
colony

U.S. Constitution
is written

American colonies
declare independence
from England

U.S. and England fight
the War of 1812

Pioneers travel West on
the Oregon Trail

U.S. fights war
with Mexico

Civil War
occurs in the
United States

UNITED STATES **HISTORY**

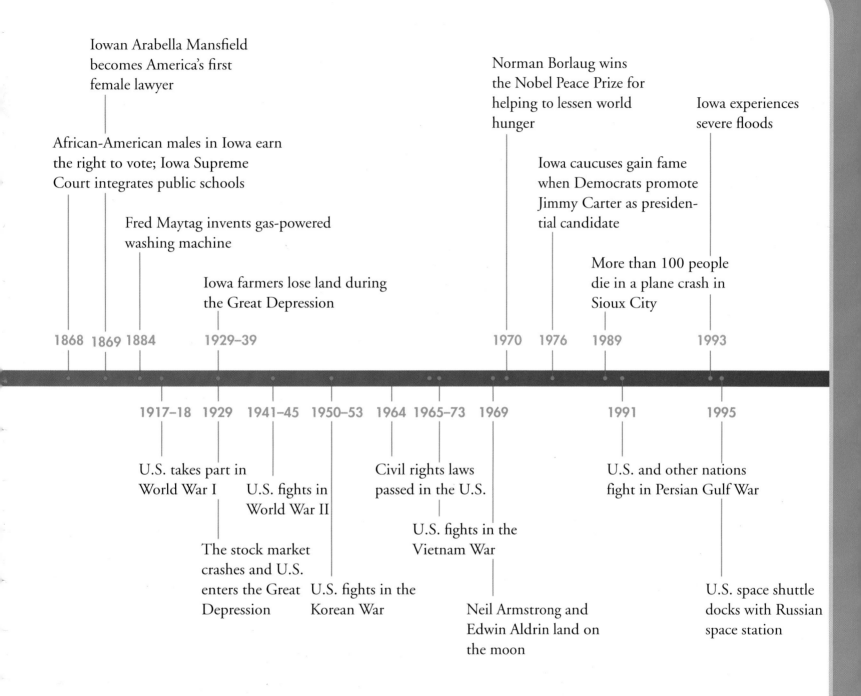

Iowan Arabella Mansfield becomes America's first female lawyer

African-American males in Iowa earn the right to vote; Iowa Supreme Court integrates public schools

Fred Maytag invents gas-powered washing machine

Iowa farmers lose land during the Great Depression

Norman Borlaug wins the Nobel Peace Prize for helping to lessen world hunger

Iowa caucuses gain fame when Democrats promote Jimmy Carter as presidential candidate

Iowa experiences severe floods

More than 100 people die in a plane crash in Sioux City

1868 1869 1884   1929–39   1970 1976 1989   1993

1917–18 1929 1941–45 1950–53 1964 1965–73 1969   1991   1995

U.S. takes part in World War I

U.S. fights in World War II

Civil rights laws passed in the U.S.

U.S. and other nations fight in Persian Gulf War

The stock market crashes and U.S. enters the Great Depression

U.S. fights in the Korean War

U.S. fights in the Vietnam War

Neil Armstrong and Edwin Aldrin land on the moon

U.S. space shuttle docks with Russian space station

GALLERY OF FAMOUS IOWANS

Amelia Jenks Bloomer
(1818–1894)
Suffragette. At a time when women always wore dresses, Bloomer started a fashion trend by wearing long, loose-fitting pants, which were eventually named "bloomers." Lived in Council Bluffs.

Norman Borlaug
(1914–)
Plant scientist who promoted creative farming techniques that helped to lessen world hunger. In 1970, he won the Nobel Peace Prize for his efforts. Born in Cresco.

Johnny Carson
(1925–)
Entertainer, comedian, and host of *The Tonight Show*. Born in Corning.

Urban "Red" Faber
(1888–1976)
Professional baseball player and later a coach for the Chicago White Sox. Born in Cascade.

Hamlin Garland
(1860–1940)
An author who wrote books about growing up on the Iowa frontier. He won the Pulitzer Prize in 1921 for his biography, *A Daughter of the Middle Border*. Lived near Osage during part of his childhood.

Arabella Mansfield
(1846–1911)
America's first licensed female lawyer. She never practiced law, but taught and served as dean at Indiana Asbury University. Mansfield also helped form the Iowa Women's Suffrage Association. Born in Burlington.

Glenn Miller
(1904–1944)
Famous bandleader of the Glenn Miller Orchestra. Also a composer and trombonist. Born in Clarinda.

John Wayne
(1907–1979)
Actor and Academy Award-winner who starred in more than 150 films, most of which were westerns. Won an Academy Award for his role in the movie *True Grit*. Born in Winterset.

Meredith Willson
(1902–1984)
Musician and composer. Wrote the hit Broadway musical *The Music Man*. He based the play on his hometown of Mason City, Iowa.

GLOSSARY

abolitionist: a person who fought against slavery

caucus: a small gathering in which members of political parties meet to vote for their party's presidential nominee

census: an official counting of the population

Civil War: the war in the United States between the Union (North) and the Confederacy (South) from 1861 to 1865; also called the War Between the States

conservation: an effort to keep the environment safe and clean

constitution: a document that outlines the laws and guiding ideas of a government

erosion: the gradual wearing away of land by water, wind, or ice

Great Depression: an economic crisis in the United States that started with the stock market crash in 1929 and continued throughout the 1930s

immigrant: a person who leaves one country to live and work in another

slavery: the practice of holding a people against their will as property of a slaveholder and forcing them to work for that slaveholder

stock market: the buying and selling of stocks

till: sand, gravel, and rocks left behind from glaciers; also called glacial drift

tuberculosis: a contagious disease of the lungs

FOR MORE INFORMATION

Web sites

Iowa's Official State Web site

www.state.ia.us/

Iowa's official state government site.

Greater Des Moines Convention and Visitors Bureau

http://www.desmoinesia.com/

What to do and see in Iowa's capital city.

Iowa Wetlands and Riparian Areas Conservation Plan Kids' Page

http://www.ag.iastate.edu/centers/iawetlands/ Kidshome.html

Information for kids about Iowa's wetlands.

What Black Hawk Did

http://members.home.net/zeldaa/bhawk.htm

More information about Chief Black Hawk.

Books

Bial, Raymond. *Amish Home.* New York, NY: Houghton Mifflin, 1993.

Bial, Raymond. *Corn Belt Harvest.* New York, NY: Houghton Mifflin, 1991.

Hiscock, Bruce. *The Big Rivers: The Missouri, The Mississippi, and the Ohio.* New York, NY: Atheneum, 1997.

Venezia, Mike. *Grant Wood (Getting to Know the World's Greatest Artists).* Danbury, CT: Children's Press, 1995.

Addresses

Iowa Division of Tourism

200 E. Grand Avenue

Des Moines, IA 50309

Office of the Governor

Iowa State Capitol

Des Moines, IA 50319

Effigy Mounds National Monument

151 Highway 76

Harpers Ferry, IA 52146

INDEX

ABOUT THE AUTHOR

Dynise Balcavage completed most of her research for this book in the library and on the Internet. She was amazed by how quickly the World Wide Web linked her office in the city of Philadelphia to the many treasures of the Hawkeye State.

A freelance writer, Balcavage is also the author of nine other books: *Ludwig van Beethoven, Steroids, The Great Chicago Fire, The Federal Bureau of Investigation, Janis Joplin, Saudi Arabia, Philip Sheridan, Gabrielle Reece*, and *Iraq*. Balcavage also frequently contributes to *Publish* magazine.

Balcavage earned a B.F.A. in visual arts from Kutztown University and an M.A. in English from Arcadia University. She lives in Philadelphia with her husband, cat, and two birds.

Photographs © 2002: AP/Wide World Photos: 42 (Jeff Beiermann), 38, 48 (Charlie Neibergall), 68 top (Buzz Orr), 16 (Brandon Pollock); Corbis Images: 74 bottom left (Scott Alonzo), 3, 9 (Tom Bean), 64 top (Bettmann), 44, 51 (Richard Cummins), 54 (Vince Streano), 33, 39, 69 (UPI), 21, 37, 74 top left; David Thoreson: 3 left, 4, 7, 11, 14, 17, 55; Dembinsky Photo Assoc.: 13 (Sharon Cummings), 58 (Mark E. Gibson), 71 bottom left (Skip Moody), 57 (G. Alan Nelson), 71 top left (George E. Stewart); Drake University Sports Information: 53; Gene Ahrens: 49, 63; H. Armstrong Roberts, Inc./J. Blank: 64; John Deere North American Agricultural Marketing Center: 41; MapQuest.com, Inc.: 70 bottom; North Wind Picture Archives: 23, 24, 26, 28, 29; Office of the Governor, Des Moines, Iowa: 70 top; Photo Researchers, NY: 8 (David R. Frazier), 43, 45 background (Norris Taylor), 71 right (Kenneth H. Thomas); Photri Inc./Lani Novak Howe: 65 bottom; State Historical Society of Iowa: 22; Stock Montage, Inc.: 19, 25, 30, 35, 36, 62, 74 right; Superstock, Inc.: 32; Tom Till: cover, 12; Visuals Unlimited: 68 bottom (Louie Bunde), 52 (Mark E. Gibson), 15 (GLE).